PIRATE QUEENS

DAUNTLESS WOMEN WHO DARED TO RULE THE HIGH SEAS

LEIGH LEWIS

Illustrated by Sara Gómez Woolley

NATIONAL
GEOGRAPHIC

WASHINGTON, D.C.

CONTENTS

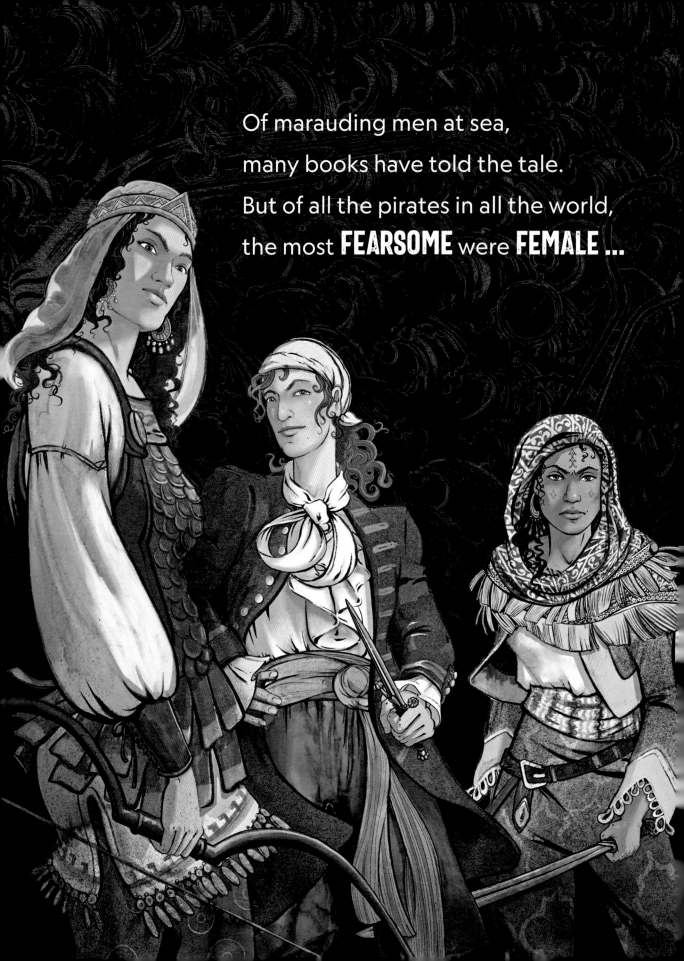

Of marauding men at sea,
many books have told the tale.
But of all the pirates in all the world,
the most **FEARSOME** were **FEMALE** ...

WHEN YOU THINK OF A PIRATE, WHO COMES TO MIND?

One evening, I took my three daughters to the local swimming pool and taught them a beloved game from my childhood—Walking the Plank. My brother and sister and I used to do just that off the diving board, taking turns as the fearsome pirate giving the command. My kids took to the game immediately, and it turned out that every pirate that came to their minds was male.

Fearsome Blackbeard, with his long, black, braided locks set aflame. Captain Hook, the fictional and dapperly dressed pirate who famously feuded with Peter Pan. And sometimes even the brash, brutish Captain Jack Sparrow, who loomed large, but only on the big screen. My girls played round after round, topping each other in both the creative commands given and the drawn-out, dramatic plunges to certain death.

Whether real or fake, fanciful or fearsome, modern or historical, male pirates have captured the imagination of children of all ages. It begs the question: Where were all the women? If you picked up this book, you may have already asked yourself this very question.

Female pirates have thrived since the dawn of piracy: penniless vagabonds and Viking warriors, governors and merchant sailors, sea captains and Islamic queens. In fact, the most powerful pirate ever to have lived was a woman named Ching Shih, who dominated the South China Sea some 200 years ago (see page 54). She reigned over 80,000 men and women, the largest pirate fleet ever assembled. (Blackbeard maxed out at 400!)

Why don't we know more about these women?

As is the case with so much of written history, female pirates have not received the same level of attention as their male counterparts. These women came from all walks of life and every corner of the globe. Their reasons for turning to piracy were as varied and complex as the women themselves: greed, adventure, pride, revenge, love, nationalism, and sometimes just the

START

lack of any other option. While stories of swashbuckling life at sea abound in romantic literature and popular movies, the truth of the matter is that pirates are often bloodthirsty, violent, callous, and cruel. This book isn't meant to glorify piracy or make pirate actions or deeds appear as heroic. Rather, it's intended to recall from history the stories some deemed not worthy of recounting, recording, or remembering because of the pirate's gender. This book is a reminder that women have made their mark in every area throughout time, even when it wasn't documented. It's a reclaiming of space for ladies who have too long been written out of history.

If not for the brief mention of female pirates in a few historical documents, we would not know about such powerful women as the avenging Islamic pirate Sayyida al Hurra. After her family was exiled during the Reconquista, a series of campaigns by Christian states to recapture what is now primarily Spain and Portugal from the Moors, she dedicated her life to making "the Christian enemy" pay. Or ruthless Grace O'Malley, who, after 40 years of plundering English ships, demanded an audience with Queen Elizabeth I (as her equal, no less) to regain her freedom. Or Artemisia I of Caria, the Greek queen and trusted adviser who double-crossed the Persian king by sinking her ally's ship to escape certain death.

After returning home from the swimming pool with my daughters that night, I started researching real-life female pirates. It turns out there were many to be discovered, and certainly many more who never made it into the history books. I vowed to do my part to fill in the gaps of feminine history, using both poetry and prose to tell the stories of some remarkable women who are often overlooked.

This book pays homage to six powerful pirates who forged their own paths, and to all of the other women in history whose stories have been lost at sea.

It's my hope that the next time someone pictures a pirate, it just may be a woman.

— Leigh Lewis

PIRATE QUEENS UNCOVERED

Swashbucklers. Scallywags. Scavengers of the seas. No matter what you call pirates, one thing is certain: They were ruthless raiders who sailed the world's oceans, stealing treasure and wreaking havoc on enemy ships. By definition, a pirate is a person who uses the sea to commit theft. Some did it for the thrill of taking treasure, or to get rich quick. Some were simply protecting their territory, while others were acquiring new territory. Some, called privateers, were hired by the government to carry out raids during wartime. Whether they were women or men, most pirates had one thing in common: While seeking their own adventures, money, and power, they sparked fear in the hearts of their rivals around the world.

So when did the first pirates pop up? Historians have traced bands of fearful seafarers all the way back to the Bronze Age, around 1200 B.C. Some 3,200 years ago, naval warriors known as the Sea Peoples would sail into Mediterranean ports, hop off their ships wielding heavy iron weapons, and pillage ancient civilizations. Noteworthy historical accounts of piracy certainly didn't stop there: Later, in 75 B.C., pirates in the Greek islands captured a then 25-year-old and Roman-emperor-to-be Julius Caesar, holding him captive for more than a month until a ransom was paid.

As time marched on, pirates continued to plunder ships and towns around the world, from Asia to the Mediterranean to Europe and beyond. Piracy reached its peak in the mid-1600s, when bands of buccaneers routinely attacked ships in seas all over. Lasting from 1660 to 1730, a period known as the Golden Age of Piracy saw now infamous grog-swilling seafarers like Blackbeard and Captain Kidd carrying out their colorful capers and terrifying attacks.

This is also when women like Anne Bonny and Mary Read made their marks in the pirating world. But we wouldn't find out about them (or those females who ruled the seas in earlier years) until many years later, since details about women pirates aren't as well known. Still, some sources do exist, and historians have used them to uncover stories about these bold female buccaneers. These are women who ruled massive fleets, wielded weapons, fought bravely in battle, and amassed massive power and wealth. And they did it all with the odds—and their societies—stacked against them.

MAKING WAVES

ARCTIC CIRCLE

90° 60° 30°W 0°

NORTH
ATLANTIC
OCEAN

N O R W

North
Sea   DENMARK

60°

IRELAND   Irish
Sea   ENGLAND

E U R

ATLANTIC
OCEAN

SPAIN

Granada

Med

Tétouan

Chefchaouen

MOROCCO

NORTH
AMERICA   Charles Town,
South Carolina

30°N

BAHAMAS

TROPIC OF CANCER

A F

JAMAICA
Caribbean Sea

PACIFIC
OCEAN

SOUTH
AMERICA

EQUATOR

CARIBBEAN

DESPITE THE TROPICAL
TEMPS AND CRYSTAL CLEAR
WATER, BONNY'S LIFE ON
THE SEA WAS ANYTHING
BUT IDYLLIC.

IRISH SEA

FOR O'MALLEY, SAILING OFF
THE RUGGED COAST OF
IRELAND MEANT NAVIGATING
ROUGH WATERS AND A
CHILLY CLIMATE.

MEDITERRANEAN

AL HURRA DOMINATED THE
WESTERN PART OF THIS SEA
WHILE DEFENDING HER
COASTAL CITY-STATE.

GENERALIZED ROUTES OF THE PIRATE QUEENS

→ Artemisia I of Caria (ca 520–460 B.C.)
→ Sela (active ca A.D. 400–420)
→ Sayyida al Hurra (ca A.D. 1485–1561)
→ Grace O'Malley (ca A.D. 1530–1603)
→ Anne Bonny (ca A.D. 1702–1782)
→ Ching Shih (ca A.D. 1775–1844)

SWEDEN

EUROPE

ASIA

N
W   E
S

GREECE
Battle of
Artemisium
Battle of
Salamis
ANATOLIA
Halicarnassus,
Caria
Mediterranean Sea

AFRICA

CHINA

30°N

Canton

VIETNAM

South China Sea

PHILIPPINES

INDIAN
OCEAN

0°

30°E   60°   90°   120°

NORTH SEA

SELA SWARMED ALMOST ANY SHIP THAT CROSSED HER PATH IN THE NORTHERN REACHES OF THE ATLANTIC OCEAN NEAR NORWAY.

MEDITERRANEAN

ARTEMISIA KEPT HER FLEETS OFF THE SHORES OF GREECE TO PROTECT HER CITY AND NEARBY ISLANDS.

PACIFIC

CHING SHIH SAILED THE SOUTH CHINA SEA, A LARGE PART OF THE PACIFIC OCEAN THAT EXTENDS TO VIETNAM, THE PHILIPPINES, AND OTHER AREAS.

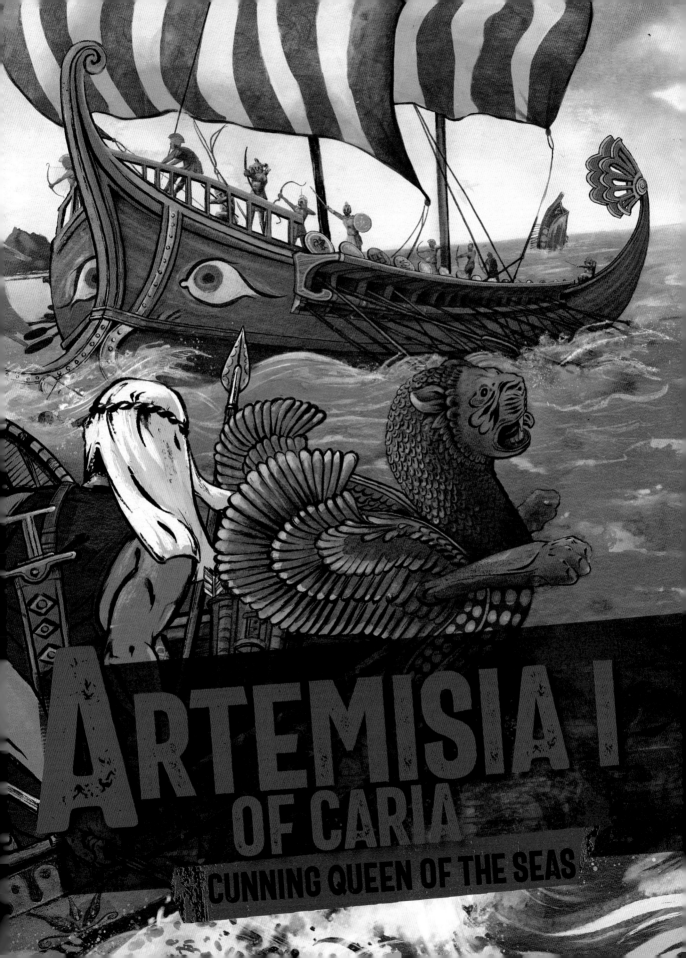

ARTEMISIA I
OF CARIA
CUNNING QUEEN OF THE SEAS

HER SEAFARING STORY

WHEN: ca 520 to 460 B.C. **WHERE:** Halicarnassus, a coastal city-state in the region of Caria in what is present-day Turkey **WHO:** A brilliant military strategist and commander, Artemisia I played a major role in the first great naval battle ever recorded in history: the Battle of Salamis between the ancient Greeks and the Persians. **ALIAS:** Artemisia I (in Greek, Αρτεμισία) aka Artemisia I of Caria aka the Queen of Halicarnassus

THE BATTLE OF SALAMIS

The King of Persia gathered up his men.
At last, he beckoned Artemisia, too.
Demanded they give counsel though he knew
his battle plan, already drawn by then.
The chorus sang the song he longed to hear,
but one discordant note rang in his ear—
"Do not attack within these tortured straits!
You lose, and Persia never rules again."
But Xerxes vetoed Artemisia's view,
demanding all prepare, proceed, pursue.
Her allies feared for Artemisia when
she claimed his plan was flawed, and dared object.
Though her enemies rejoiced at her sure fate,
she spoke the truth and won the king's respect.

Soon Artemisia gamely prepped for war
as Xerxes safely viewed it from his throne,
at ease, for his advantage was well known,
with twice the ships and thrice the men or more.
But Greece's winning triremes set the pace.
And rushing! Raiding! Ramming! They gave chase.
Now Artemisia fled from them until
her path was blocked. Alas, she seemed done for.
In her way, a ship of Persia's own!
Now trapped. And doomed! But then, her mettle shone
when, though it wasn't visible from shore,
she sank her ally, clinching Xerxes' loss.
Though he heaped praise on Artemisia still,
history shows the King was double-crossed.

THE COMMANDING QUEEN

ARTEMISIA'S RISE TO FAME AS THE FIRST KNOWN FEMALE ADMIRAL

ARTEMISIA'S TALE IS OF A **FIERCE WARRIOR AND RULER** WITH TRUE SKILL ON THE SEA.

CARIA WAS AN ANCIENT, AFFLUENT CITY-STATE, THEN PART OF THE PERSIAN EMPIRE, AND ARTEMISIA WAS ITS QUEEN. SHE WAS **A BOLD AND BRAVE LEADER** WHO SUCCESSFULLY COMMANDED SEVERAL SHIPS THROUGH SOME OF THE MOST SIGNIFICANT BATTLES OF HER TIME.

STEPPING UP

Much of what we know about Artemisia is plucked from the works of Herodotus, the ancient Greek writer known as the father of history. He tells of a gutsy queen who first took over the throne after her husband, the king of Caria, died. As a young widow and single mom of a grown-up son, Artemisia stepped up—and staked her claim in Caria.

A QUEEN AND A WARRIOR

Artemisia's main mission? Seeking allies to safeguard her land. During a time of near constant conflict between the Greeks and the Persians, she became an ally of Xerxes, the king of Persia, who accepted Artemisia as a commander in the Persian navy. While it was unusual for a sitting queen to lead her soldiers to battle, she gamely took charge of a fleet of ships— and boldly braved the bloody scene.

TRICKS UP HER SLEEVE

Artemisia's first test on the water came during the Battle of Artemisium, a spat between Greek and Persian fleets over territory. A true tactician, the cunning queen is said to have carried both the Greek *and* Persian flags aboard her ship. She'd raise the Greek flag as she came upon unsuspecting enemy ships. They'd think she was an approaching ally—until she'd unleash

ARTEMISIA'S NAME COMES FROM ARTEMIS, THE ANCIENT GREEK GODDESS OF WILDERNESS AND HUNTING.

AN UNCOLLECTED REWARD

Not only could Artemisia outwit her enemies at sea, she was able to elude them on land as well. After Artemisia's antics during the Battle of Artemisium, which fueled their anger over a woman being able to outsmart them at sea, the Greeks put a bounty on her head. And it wasn't just a pittance of a payment: They offered up to 10,000 drachmas for her capture. That was a payout large enough to pay the salaries of 28 workers for an entire year! But the threat remained only that—a threat. Artemisia was never captured, and the reward remained uncollected.

a surprise attack. This tricky tactic gave the Persians an edge in the battle. After three days of fighting, the Greeks retreated.

A WISE WARNING

However, the real battle was just beginning. Next up: a clash near Salamis, a tiny island close to Athens, Greece. Fresh off the Persians' tactical victory at Artemisium, an uber-confident Xerxes burned Athens to the ground and made plans to launch another naval attack to nail his enemies once and for all. But Artemisia advised otherwise. Unlike the male commanders, she had the courage to speak her mind to the king. Warning that "our enemies are much stronger in the sea than us," she encouraged him to attack on land instead. Determined to sink the Greeks at sea, Xerxes ignored her advice and went with the majority view of his male commanders. He moved forward with the mission, bringing his talented commander along.

A MASTERFUL MOVE

Even with her reservations, Artemisia loyally guided her ship into battle. Here, she pulled off one of her most masterful moves yet. Trapped between allied ships and an enemy Greek ship in hot pursuit, Artemisia made the split-second decision to ram right into her allies. Seeing this unfold, the Greeks stopped chase, assuming the ship was on their side.

THE QUEEN KNOWS BEST

Artemisia's warning to avoid a naval battle proved prophetic. Despite her heroic efforts, the Greeks dominated the Persians in the narrow waterway between Athens and Salamis. While the Persians never quite recovered from this major blow, Artemisia emerged as one of the wisest and wittiest commanders to ever bring a ship to battle.

Xerxes I had a bridge built for his army to march over the sea to invade Greece. When rough waters demolished the bridge, Xerxes punished the sea by whipping it with a chain 300 times.

WHAT'S IN A NAME?

Plenty, if you consider that Artemisia was named after Artemis, the Greek goddess of wilderness and hunting. And she wore the name well: Not only did Artemisia share with the goddess a love of archery and the thrill of the chase, she was also equally exceptional at breaking down gender barriers.

According to myth, Artemis showed incredible smarts, strength, and courage from birth. (She even helped her mom deliver her twin brother, Apollo, moments after taking her first breath!) While Artemisia may not have pulled off such a, well, godly feat, she was equally witty, brash, and bold in real life. In fact, Herodotus was so impressed by Artemisia's prowess at sea that he used the Greek word *andreia* to describe her. Referring to someone who possesses the virtue of courage, this term was usually reserved for men. That Herodotus wrote about her at all is a sign that she was a force to be reckoned with, since it was very uncommon for a man to document anything about a woman back then. Even more impressive? Artemisia's name was included in Herodotus's writing, but her husband's was not.

SELA

A DEFIANT OLDER SISTER

HER SEAFARING STORY

WHEN: Active ca A.D. 400 to 420 **WHERE:** Norway **WHO:** Sister to Koller, the ruler of Norway, Sela set out for a life of adventure in piracy. Rather than be ruled by her brother, she took to the seas to torment him.

I WILL BE QUEEN*

SELA   **KOLLER**

I reject this royal rejection!
Father chose son, not daughter. The proper selection.

But I'm older. And bolder! The rightful heir.
Silly sister, who told you life was fair?

This isn't over. You will see ...
... see the whole world bow before me?

You're not fit to be king!
Kiss my ring! You should be glad!

For this? Are you mad?
You're a Princess.

So what? I just sit here and wave?
Is that so hard? Yes, girl, BEHAVE!

And you? What is your fate?
I'll rule at sea. Oceans await!

My advice? Watch your back.
No need. I'm on track.

But Koller—
You MUST call me KING!

I've never seen you look smaller.
I could have your head.

I'll have MY way. I'll see YOU dead.
You're just bitter, sister.

Not bitter. Better! I'll be coming for you.
And what exactly would you do?

I'll pillage and plunder ...
With what skills, I wonder?

A crew at my call ...
... who will laugh as you fall.

I'll grow stronger ... and faster ...
... yet I'll still be your master.

I'll conquer the seas!
You'll DO as I please!

Take captives and treasure.
YOU SERVE AT MY PLEASURE!

One day soon, you'll never know which ...
You? Surprise ME? Now that's rich.

I'll come for you, quietly ...
You'll do something? Finally?

Put my sword to your neck ...
I'll be waiting on deck.

... and in the end, I'LL wear the ring.
SISTER, I AM YOUR KING!

I AM MORE THAN YOUR SISTER! I AM SELA ... AND I WILL BE QUEEN!

*The historian Saxo Grammaticus, who penned Sela's fifth-century story some 800 years later, erroneously called her a princess and her brother a king, though Norway wouldn't have kings, queens, and princesses until the ninth century. This poem thus uses the same terminology as the historical source for Sela.

NORWAY'S MOST NOTORIOUS

WHEN IT COMES TO WOMEN PIRATES, **SELA WAS A PIONEER.**

EXPERTS SAY SHE IS ONE OF THE **EARLIEST KNOWN PIRATES,** HAVING RULED THE SEAS SOME 1,600 YEARS AGO.

WHILE THE DETAILS OF SELA'S REIGN ARE SKETCHY—WHAT WE KNOW OF HER COMES FROM THE ACCOUNTS OF ONE 13TH-CENTURY DANISH HISTORIAN— HER TALE IS BOTH TRIUMPHANT AND TRAGIC.

OH, BROTHER

Sibling rivalry was alive and well back in the fifth century—at least when it came to the Norwegian elites. Simply put, Sela did not get along with her brother, Koller. When he rose to power as the ruler of Norway, Sela turned to a rebellious life on the seas instead.

TREASURE SEEKER

Sela set her sights on ships sailing the North Atlantic Ocean, plundering any vessel that crossed her path. An experienced sailor, Sela had no trouble navigating the seas, and her attacks on other ships were swift and successful. As a result, she quickly collected a stash of treasures and massive wealth—as well as a reputation as a fierce warrior.

A MASTER PLAN

As the saying goes, money can't buy you happiness. No matter how much bling Sela snapped up from other ships, she couldn't shake her hatred for her brother. This was even more true once Koller took up pirating as well and became all consumed with controlling the seas.

Sela set out to cut off Koller's power. Upon hearing of his plan to wage war on Horwendil, a formidable fellow pirate of whom Koller was bitterly jealous, Sela

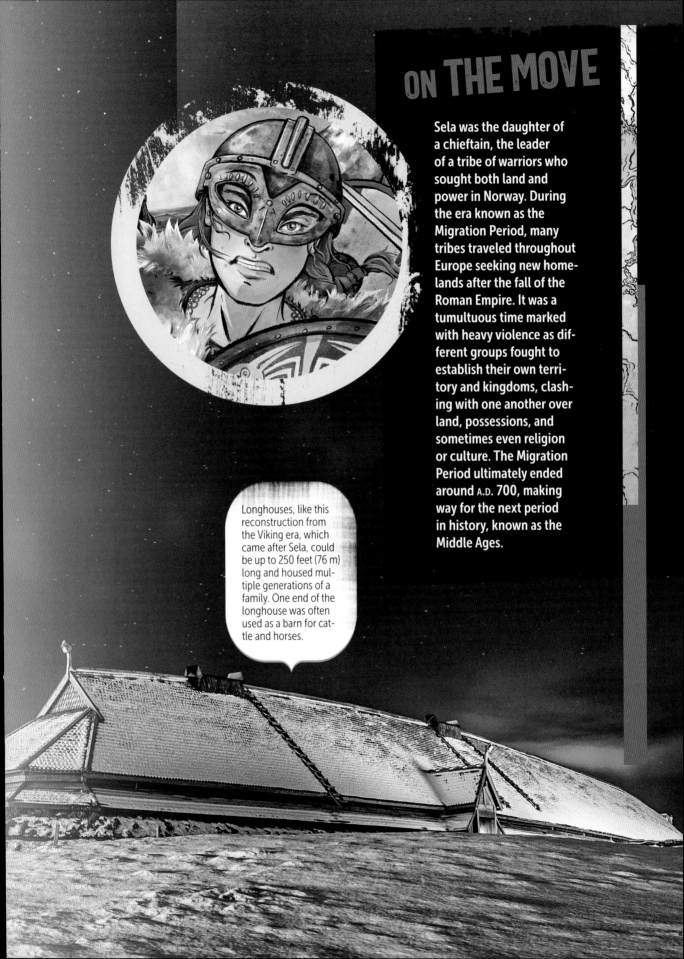

ON THE MOVE

Sela was the daughter of a chieftain, the leader of a tribe of warriors who sought both land and power in Norway. During the era known as the Migration Period, many tribes traveled throughout Europe seeking new homelands after the fall of the Roman Empire. It was a tumultuous time marked with heavy violence as different groups fought to establish their own territory and kingdoms, clashing with one another over land, possessions, and sometimes even religion or culture. The Migration Period ultimately ended around A.D. 700, making way for the next period in history, known as the Middle Ages.

Longhouses, like this reconstruction from the Viking era, which came after Sela, could be up to 250 feet (76 m) long and housed multiple generations of a family. One end of the longhouse was often used as a barn for cattle and horses.

raced to attack her brother and his fleet first. But she arrived too late. By the time she caught up with Koller near a deserted island in the Atlantic, he had already set off on foot to find Horwendil. It turned out the two met up and engaged in an epic sword fight, with Horwendil lopping off Koller's leg. The injury proved fatal, and Koller met his demise at the hands of Horwendil.

STILL A THREAT

Sela was never able to enjoy the fall of her sibling rival. In fact, she had sailed right into extremely dangerous territory. After all, given her reputation as a powerful pirate, Sela was just as much a threat to Horwendil as she had been to her brother. As if killing the king wasn't savage enough, Horwendil murdered Sela, Koller's sister, as well. (Ironically, years later, Horwendil would be killed by *his* own brother, Fengo, who was consumed by jealousy of his sibling.)

While Sela did not rule the seas for long, her legacy lingers. Centuries after her time, this powerful woman is still remembered for her daring raids—and her relentless spirit.

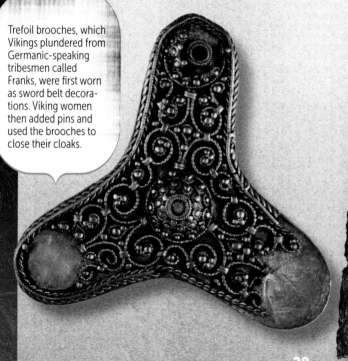

Trefoil brooches, which Vikings plundered from Germanic-speaking tribesmen called Franks, were first worn as sword belt decorations. Viking women then added pins and used the brooches to close their cloaks.

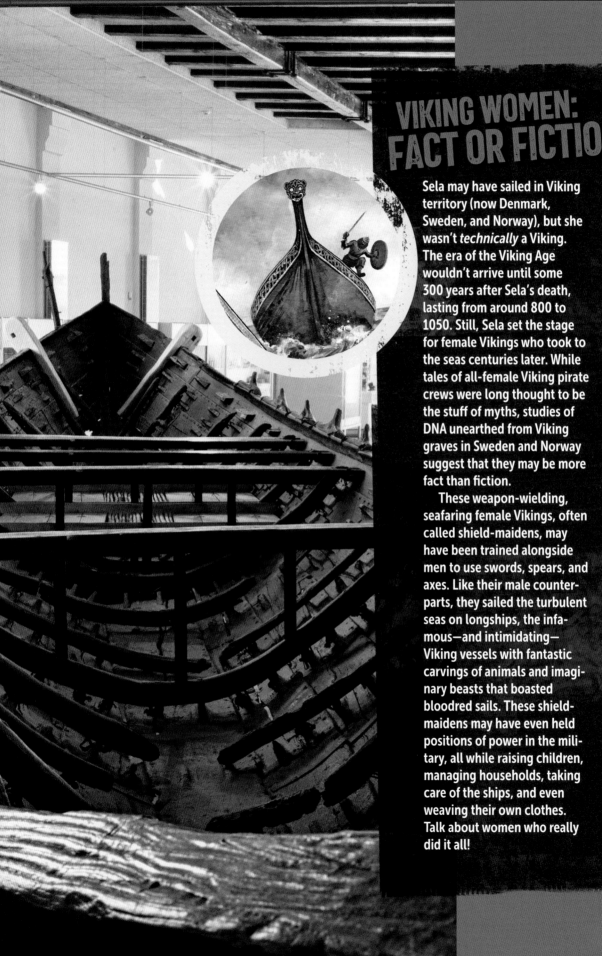

VIKING WOMEN: FACT OR FICTION?

Sela may have sailed in Viking territory (now Denmark, Sweden, and Norway), but she wasn't *technically* a Viking. The era of the Viking Age wouldn't arrive until some 300 years after Sela's death, lasting from around 800 to 1050. Still, Sela set the stage for female Vikings who took to the seas centuries later. While tales of all-female Viking pirate crews were long thought to be the stuff of myths, studies of DNA unearthed from Viking graves in Sweden and Norway suggest that they may be more fact than fiction.

These weapon-wielding, seafaring female Vikings, often called shield-maidens, may have been trained alongside men to use swords, spears, and axes. Like their male counter-parts, they sailed the turbulent seas on longships, the infa-mous—and intimidating— Viking vessels with fantastic carvings of animals and imaginary beasts that boasted bloodred sails. These shield-maidens may have even held positions of power in the mili-tary, all while raising children, managing households, taking care of the ships, and even weaving their own clothes. Talk about women who really did it all!

SAYYIDA AL HURRA

A REVENGE-SEEKING QUEEN

HER SEAFARING STORY

WHEN: ca A.D. 1485 to 1561 **WHERE:** Mediterranean Sea **WHO:** A fierce defender of her Moroccan city, Sayyida al Hurra is considered one of the most important female figures in the modern western Islamic world **ALIAS:** Sayyida al Hurra (in Arabic, السيدة الحرة) aka Lalla Aisha bint Ali ibn Rashid al-Alami aka the Queen of Tétouan. Her name can be loosely translated from Arabic as "lady who is free and independent."

KISMET

Dreams of Mama laughing as sweet treats flee her skirt pocket—pomegranates again!
Daylight makes her gasp, grasp at fading memories of Spain. Awoke too late again.

They come for her religion, her history, her home. All that she has ever known.
Isn't God by any other name still God? She'd never question her fate again.

Piracy is a game of power, of strategy, of irresistible lures.
The cleverest captor quietly lies in wait as her foes take the bait again.

She does not forgive. She cannot forget. She fights the fight for all those forced to flee.
One day, her evil enemies will pay. Her life, to this she dedicates again.

"Oh, Barbarossa—You rise in the East, I'll set in the West. Kismet, my brother!"
With these words, she makes the sea such impossible waters to navigate again.

Fog clears. Looking ahead, Sayyida, Queen of Tétouan, envisions the last move.
Trap the King. Inshallah, fortune foretold is fortune realized. Checkmate again.

She chooses to capture, not kill. "Come! Save your people. For a fee, let them go free!"
A pillager with principles and purpose. Open to negotiate again.

"Destined to ascend in rank." "Avenger of the Exiled." "The Last Islamic Queen."
Expectations high as heaven. Shoulders pulled back, chin up, she bears this weight again.

The Sultan of Fez proposes. No man more powerful. "Yes," she says, "On these terms:
We marry here. YOU come to ME. Leaving my home is not up for debate again."

Her real name was ... Lalla? Or maybe Aisha. Her title: **Sayyida al Hurra**.
Honored Queen. By any name, she rules. Her supremacy she'll demonstrate again.

HER story is not captured like his story, as HIStory. Demand its future.
Female pirates thrived: Freebooters! Corsairs! She-sea-dogs! Set the record straight again.

THE GREAT AVENGER

THE WESTERN MEDITERRANEAN'S UNDISPUTED PIRATE QUEEN

CHASED OUT OF HER CHILDHOOD HOME BECAUSE OF HER **FAMILY'S RELIGION,** SAYYIDA AL HURRA ROSE ABOVE THE HATE TO BRAVELY LEAD THE **COASTAL CITY-STATE OF TÉTOUAN** IN THE AFRICAN COUNTRY OF MOROCCO AND TO DOMINATE THE WESTERN MEDITERRANEAN SEA.

Under Sayyida al Hurra's rule, Tétouan prospered, largely from gold, goods, and other treasures seized during attacks on Portuguese and Spanish ships.

A SUDDEN CHANGE

Picture this: You're seven years old, living a lovely life with your well-off family in Granada, a city in southern Spain. Suddenly, everything you've ever known is stripped away as your family is forced to flee your idyllic existence. This is the story of a young girl named Aisha—later known as Sayyida al Hurra—who grew up to become a ruthless leader set on seeking revenge.

MAKING IT WORK IN MOROCCO

Around 1500, Spain's rulers, King Ferdinand and Queen Isabella, began forcing all Muslims out in order to create a Catholic-dominated country. This pushed an entire population of refugees into regions that included the Rif Mountains of northern Morocco in Africa, where Aisha's family eventually settled. Her childhood in Morocco was a happy one. Her father was a tribal chief of the city-state of Chefchaouen, and she received a top-notch education from leading scholars, mastering new languages, including Spanish and Portuguese. Still, Aisha never forgot how her family was forced out of their first home in Spain. She wanted revenge on behalf of all mistreated refugees.

PIRATE FASHION

Did real-life pirates actually have hooks for hands or sport a black patch over one eye? The pirates we see in popular culture often do, but here's the truth behind some of the trends.

Captain Hook's one-arm look may have been inspired by Sayyida's partner in crime, a fearsome figure named Oruç Reis, Barbarossa. Reis led attacks on Spanish colonies, merchant trading ships, and even ships that belonged to the pope. Having lost an arm in battle, Oruç in fact wore a silver prosthetic arm.

PATCH WORK

At least one actual pirate is known to have rocked an eye patch. His name was Rahmah ibn Jabir ibn Adhbi Al Jalhami, an Arab ruler who sailed the Persian Gulf in the early 1800s. Diseases and accidents during this time could cause eye loss, a likely reason to sport a patch.

A NEW LEADER

Around 1501, Aisha married Abu Hassan al-Mandari, the governor of nearby city-state Tétouan. Once a major seaport in the area, Tétouan had been all but abandoned after being destroyed during war. Treated as an equal by her husband, Aisha became co-ruler and led the revitalization of the struggling seaport. She returned Tétouan to a thriving metropolis complete with a mosque where all Muslims could worship. By the time her husband passed away, Aisha had established herself as a well-respected leader. Given the title "Sayyida al Hurra," which loosely translates from Arabic as "lady who is free and independent," she continued to propel Tétouan toward prominence for another 25 years.

A POWERFUL ALLIANCE

Sayyida's past still haunted her. Committed to standing up for all Muslims, she sought out the Barbary pirates, who had been raiding Christian-controlled seaports and coastal villages. Their leader, Oruç Reis, who became known as Barbarossa, recognized Sayyida as a peer, and he agreed to split reign of the sea. With a fleet of sleek ships, a crew of savage soldiers, and the support of one of the most fearsome pirates alive, Sayyida took over the western Mediterranean. She purposefully plundered Spanish and Christian ships, stealing their money and valuables to fund Tétouan and exact her revenge.

A MOSTLY HAPPY ENDING

And so, the little girl who grew up fearing the Spanish became a woman who ignited fear in those who once oppressed her people. Sayyida's dominance on the sea—and as the leader of Tétouan—lasted until around 1542, when she was overthrown by her son-in-law. Forced into retirement, the story goes that she returned to her former home in the mountains of Morocco, where she peacefully spent the rest of her life. She was the last woman to hold the title of "al Hurra." Today, Sayyida ranks among the most important Islamic female figures in history.

King Ferdinand and Queen Isabella expelled Muslim and Jewish families from Granada, ending nearly 800 years of Muslim rule in the Iberian Peninsula. Barbarossa, pictured above, and Sayyida ultimately took revenge.

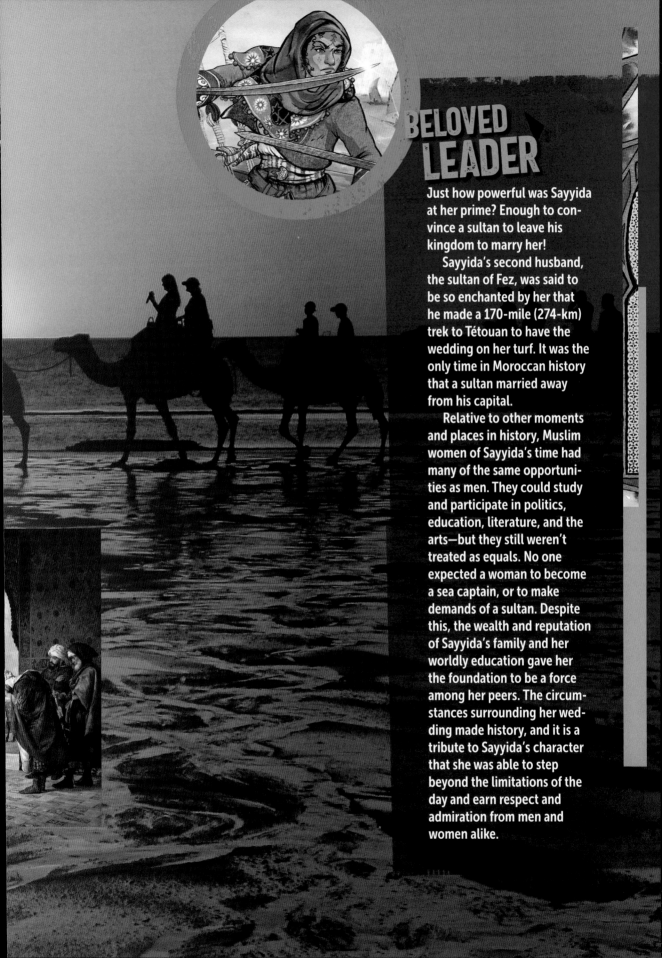

BELOVED LEADER

Just how powerful was Sayyida at her prime? Enough to convince a sultan to leave his kingdom to marry her!

Sayyida's second husband, the sultan of Fez, was said to be so enchanted by her that he made a 170-mile (274-km) trek to Tétouan to have the wedding on her turf. It was the only time in Moroccan history that a sultan married away from his capital.

Relative to other moments and places in history, Muslim women of Sayyida's time had many of the same opportunities as men. They could study and participate in politics, education, literature, and the arts—but they still weren't treated as equals. No one expected a woman to become a sea captain, or to make demands of a sultan. Despite this, the wealth and reputation of Sayyida's family and her worldly education gave her the foundation to be a force among her peers. The circumstances surrounding her wedding made history, and it is a tribute to Sayyida's character that she was able to step beyond the limitations of the day and earn respect and admiration from men and women alike.

GRACE O'MALLEY
THE FEARLESS SEAFARER

HER SEAFARING STORY

WHEN: ca A.D. 1530 to 1603 **WHERE:** Ireland **WHO:** A warrior from Ireland who became a fearsome opponent to the British realm **ALIAS:** Grace O'Malley aka Gráinne Ní Mháille aka Gráinne Mhaol

PETITION TO QUEEN ELIZABETH I

Unto Her Majesty, The Queen of England, Elizabeth I

My legend no doubt seeps through
    the cracks of your castle
as yours sweeps wide 'cross every
    sea.

Whispers of my ways carry in the
    wind:
That I battled a band of eagles to
save the O'Malley sheep,
talon marks forever marring my
    brow.
That my father deemed my flowing
    mane
a curse on his ship
so I sliced it off with a sword.
Grace the Bald, they call me still.
That I birthed my son below deck,
    then
ascended to thwart an attack by
    Turkish corsairs.

Is not your legacy beset by rumor as
    well?
You're a murderer! Or more, a man!

Fact and fiction blend when
spewed from the mouths of men
who wish us dead.
At war against me is but one such
    man,
hell-bent on my ruin.

My sole sources of income, cattle and
    horses?
He commandeered.

My sanctuary, my home?
He destroyed.
My blood, my beloved sons?
He murdered one and imprisoned
    another.
He believes I plunder for pleasure,
yet he sabotaged all other means of
    survival.

He pursues me as if God himself declared
    me the devil.
But God had no hand in this charade.

It was you.

You, Your Majesty, who sicced Sir Richard
    Bingham on me.
You who unleashed his misplaced fury,
though who could have foreseen his
ruthless conviction or ruinous ways?

I beg of you, grant me freedom and
I shall become your fiercest ally.
Sure as we share these fiery locks
and the crowns on our heads,
let us unite to address your "quarrel with
    all the world."
Call off your sea dog. Free my son. Allow
    me a life.

See yourself in me, and me in you.
Have mercy.

Gráinne Ní Mháille

GRACE AND GRIT

WITH UNRIVALED SAILING SKILLS AND A DEEP KNOWLEDGE OF THE WATERS AROUND IRELAND, O'MALLEY RULED THE WAVES BY USING THE NOOKS AND CRANNIES OF THE COUNTRY'S COAST-LINE TO HIDE FROM ENEMIES AND TO ESCAPE SHIPS SHE'D PLUNDERED.

LIKE FATHER, LIKE DAUGHTER

Grace O'Malley grew up wanting to be just like her dad, lord of the powerful seafaring O'Malley clan. The only problem? During the 16th century, it was believed girls didn't belong at sea. Her dad, known as "Black Oak," was sure Grace's long hair would catch in the ship's ropes, endangering his crew. What did Grace do? She took a knife and chopped off her fiery red hair and pretended to be a boy to gain access to her father's ship. Her father discovered her disguise and caved in, allowing her to stay aboard—as long as she was willing to work hard to become a strong sailor. Her new nickname? Grace the Bald.

A CALCULATING COMMANDER

O'Malley's time on the water with her dad and his crew gave her the skills, grit, and courage to command her own fleet. But she wouldn't be able to assume solo control just yet. At 16, O'Malley married the son of the leader of a neighboring clan, with whom she later had three children, two sons and a daughter. When her husband was killed in an ambush by a rival clan, she seized the opportunity to return to the sea.

"Men fight wars. Women win them."

—*Queen Elizabeth I of England*

42

QUEEN ELIZABETH'S
LIFE OF PIRACY

England had a reputation for piracy long before Queen Elizabeth I took the throne in 1558. While the queen was not a sailor, she understood naval combat and commanded a fleet that prided itself on its skills at sea.

Queen Elizabeth I could not officially endorse piracy, but she quickly realized that privateers, or pirates working for a government, could raise the money she needed to build her empire. Called "sea dogs," these pirates played a key role in the 1588 defeat of the Spanish Armada, a fleet of 130 Spanish ships that was on a mission to overthrow the queen.

Wasting no time, O'Malley masterminded a trading network to Spain and Portugal and led raids on any vessel that came close to her shores. Soon, she was commanding a fleet of ships with as many as 200 men under her watch, eventually claiming ultimate rule over her clan's coastal region in Irish waters.

NEXT STEPS

In 1567, O'Malley further boosted her power by marrying Richard Bourke, the owner of a large fleet of trading vessels—and an impressive castle where she could keep her fleet and crew. Whether O'Malley married Bourke for love or for loot isn't certain, but they split up after just one year. (O'Malley is said to have famously tossed Bourke's belongings outside his castle gates, publicly dismissing him.) Still, the two became pirating partners, as well as parents to a son named Theobald. Legend has it that O'Malley gave birth to her son while on a trading expedition. A few hours later, her ship was attacked by Turkish corsairs, and Grace rose from below deck, gun in hand, to join the fight.

CUTTING A DEAL WITH A QUEEN

After many prosperous years pirating, O'Malley's fortunes had taken a turn. With one son murdered and another kidnapped, and no means to support herself, she was nearly out of options. Imagine the bravery it must have taken to approach none other than Queen Elizabeth I, England's ruler. Against all odds, the queen responded to O'Malley's letter, arranging a meeting. When they met, they agreed that England—which had conquered Ireland—would return O'Malley's son if O'Malley promised to switch teams and pirate for the English, not against them. Which she did, briefly. But pirating for the enemy soon grew old, and O'Malley returned to plundering for the Irish.

O'Malley is believed to have died in 1603—the same year as Queen Elizabeth I. Today, for her legacy of fierce opposition to British rule, O'Malley is remembered through Irish songs and legends, many of which illustrate her courage and daring exploits on the sea.

In 1593, O'Malley met Queen Elizabeth and refused to bow. Not only was O'Malley not the queen's subject, but she herself was a queen and considered herself an equal.

ANTHOLOGIA HIBERNICA.
VOL. II.

GRANA UILE introduced to QUEEN Elizabeth.

W. Beauford delin

Clayton sculp

BEATING A
BITTER RIVAL

There wasn't much of anything—or anyone—that O'Malley couldn't handle. But she nearly met her match in Sir Richard Bingham, an English soldier and naval commander who served under Queen Elizabeth I during the conquest of Ireland. In an effort to obliterate O'Malley's power and resolve, Bingham, as governor of Connaught, ordered the murder of her oldest son as well as the kidnapping of another son. He also took control of O'Malley's castle, confiscated her land, stole her cattle, and even sailed off with her fleet.

O'Malley refused to be defeated. As a last resort, she famously traveled to England to meet with Queen Elizabeth. Bingham tried to convince the queen to ignore O'Malley, but the monarch made time for her anyway. Elizabeth was impressed by the bold Irishwoman and respected her wishes. As for Bingham? He was ordered to safely return O'Malley's son to Ireland, as well as all of her goods and land. With her disgraced rival stripped of power, O'Malley regained her foothold as a fierce and unforgettable leader.

ANNE BONNY

SNEAKY TACTICIAN AND BRAVE FIGHTER

HER SEAFARING STORY

WHEN: ca A.D. 1702 to 1782 **WHERE:** Caribbean Sea **WHO:** One of the most famous seafaring females in history, Anne Bonny had a pirating career that was short but savage.

THE ENDLESS FIGHT

From the time she was born,
that girl loved a fight.
Anyone dare cross her
felt the full force of Anne's might.
Had to treat her right,
or bear the consequence.
Try to crush her confidence
or touch her wrong
or dim her light?
With competence,
and fists
and knives,
Anne would teach them a lesson all right,
give 'em the fight of their lives.

At sixteen years old,
Anne decided to flee,
ditched her daddy's plantation
for a life at sea,
married James Bonny,
but found out that he
was not a real pirate, just a mere privateer.
That's when she decided to disappear.

Took up with a true Captain—Jack—
and learned to ambush, adapt, attack.
Dressed like a man, cutlass in hand,
she battled advancing pirates back.

Anne was wonderstruck by another:
Mark Read, skilled and scary.
Only Anne knew that Mark was actually Mary—
her *sister*-in-arms, not her brother.
They mobilized and terrorized
undaunted
until Anne finally realized
she had the life she always wanted.

That is,
until Jack and the whole male crew,
celebrating their pirated plunder,
fell asleep below deck,
down under,
while their ship was taken over.
Up top, Anne and Mary fought gallantly,
but the whole crew was captured,
    tragically,
then tried and sentenced
to die.

THE END.

Except ...
facing their own mortality,
they,
Anne and Mary,
both pregnant,
fended for their lives—
"pleaded the belly"—
and were given a stay.

Once freed,
Anne made her way to the gallows,
death lurking in the shadows,
to launch a (verbal) attack,
this one last time on cowardly Jack.
A spiteful plan—
she leaned in close, not for a kiss,
but to whisper this
venomous epilogue:

"Had you fought like a man,
you need not be hanged like a dog."

RUTHLESS AT SEA

ANNE BONNY, A REAL-LIFE PIRATE OF THE CARIBBEAN

MOVE OVER, JACK SPARROW: ONE OF **THE DEADLIEST PIRATES OF THE CARIBBEAN** WAS ACTUALLY AN IRISH TEEN NAMED ANNE CORMAC BONNY.

BONNY'S TIME RULING THE SEA MAY HAVE ONLY LASTED A FEW MONTHS, BUT SHE LEFT A **PERMANENT MARK IN PIRACY LORE.**

TEMPER, TEMPER

Anne Bonny was born in Ireland and raised in the American colonies. The tales of her bad-girl behavior begin when she was just a tween. Legend has it that, at 13, she beat up a boy so badly that he "lay ill for a considerable time." Three years later, she was said to have tested her temper on her father when he disapproved of her wedding to a penniless sailor named James Bonny. Anne's father disowned her; she supposedly burned his plantation to the ground. Needless to say, you wouldn't want to get on Bonny's bad side.

ON BOARD

Alongside her new husband, Bonny sailed from Charleston, South Carolina—then known as Charles Town—for the Bahamas around 1718. It was there that she first plunged into piracy when she met John "Calico Jack" Rackham, the charismatic captain of a pirate ship. Bonny fell in love with Rackham and ran

John Rackham, aka Calico Jack, is often credited with designing the iconic pirate flag commonly called the Jolly Roger, which bears a skull and crossed swords.

PIRATING RULES

Pirate crews may not have cared much about laws, but that didn't mean they were without rules. After an 18th-century pirate, Bartholomew Roberts, died, a written copy of his ship's charter turned up. Here are some of his "do's and don'ts."

DO blow your candles out by 8 p.m.

DON'T cheat on your mates. Otherwise, you'll be left stranded.

DO vote in the ship's affairs.

DON'T allow women on the ship or on the crew. Breaking this rule is punishable by death.

DO take a rest day on Sunday ... *only* if you're one of the ship's musicians. (Regular crewmembers get no days off.)

off to be part of his crew, disguising herself as a man to all but him. She helped raise the sails, heave up the anchor, and load their essentials and their riches, including crops such as cacao beans. And, of course, Bonny was quick to take up arms when raiding other vessels they pursued in and around Jamaica.

GIRL POWER

During these plundering voyages, the crew was joined by Mary Read, who also had been flying under the radar while posing as a man. She teamed up with Anne Bonny, and they fought side by side. Wearing flowing jackets, long pants, and scarves wrapped around their heads, Read and Bonny wielded weapons like cutlasses and pistols while leading raids of several boats. Once, they captured an enemy boat's crew and held them captive for days.

But the looting didn't last long. One autumn night in 1720, as Read and Bonny hung out on the deck of Calico Jack's ship, the *William*, a mysterious ship pulled up alongside them. The governor of Jamaica had sent the boat to pursue the pirate ship and to demand that the *William* crew surrender. The two women refused and sprang into action instead, firing their pistols and swinging their swords. They put up a good fight but were ultimately overpowered. The entire *William* crew was taken prisoner in Jamaica and sentenced to death.

Bonny and Read were eventually spared. Why? Both were pregnant, and the law at the time stated that a woman "with child" should be sentenced after their babies were born. Before that could happen, Read died of a fever and Bonny disappeared. The story goes that she either moved back to South Carolina and eventually had eight more children, or that she escaped to another Caribbean island, changed her name to Annabelle, and lived out the rest of her days.

A GENERAL
HISTORY
OF THE *Galton*
Robberies and Murders
Of the most notorious
PYRATES,
AND ALSO
Their *Policies*, *Discipline* and *Government*,
From their firſt RISE and SETTLEMENT in the Iſland of *Providence*, in 1717, to the preſent Year 1724.

WITH
The remarkable ACTIONS and ADVENTURES of the two Female Pyrates, *Mary Read* and *Anne Bonny*.

To which is prefix'd
An ACCOUNT of the famous Captain *Avery* and his Companions; with the Manner of his Death in *England*.

The Whole digeſted into the following CHAPTERS;

Chap. I. Of Captain *Avery*.	VIII. Of Captain *England*.
II. The Riſe of Pyrates.	IX. Of Captain *Davis*.
III. Of Captain *Martel*.	X. Of Captain *Roberts*.
IV. Of Captain *Bonnet*.	XI. Of Captain *Worley*.
V. Of Captain *Thatch*.	XII. Of Captain *Lowther*.
VI. Of Captain *Vane*.	XIII. Of Captain *Low*.
VII. Of Captain *Rackam*.	XIV. Of Captain *Evans*.

And their ſeveral Crews.

To which is added,
A ſhort ABSTRACT of the Statute and Civil Law, in Relation to PYRACY.

By Captain CHARLES JOHNSON.

LONDON, Printed for *Ch. Rivington* at the *Bible* and *Crown* in St. *Paul's Church-Yard*, *J. Lacy* at the *Ship* near the *Temple-Gate*, and *J. Stone* next the *Crown* Coffee-houſe the back of *Greys-Inn*, 1724.

Much of what we know about Anne Bonny comes from a biography of pirates called *A General History of the Pyrates* by Captain Charles Johnson, which many believe is an alias for *Robinson Crusoe* author Daniel Defoe.

VERY SUPERSTITIOUS

Why were women shunned from most pirate ships? It has to do with a persistent superstition that females brought bad luck on board by distracting the sailors from their sea duties. Many pirates took this myth as the truth, which is why women like Anne Bonny and Mary Read had to sneak aboard ships masquerading as men.

And it wasn't just women who were believed to bring bad luck: Another superstition suggested that bananas should not be brought on board. This myth may have started in the 1700s when several ships in the Caribbean, all carrying cargo of bananas, disappeared. Not only that, but fishermen were said to inexplicably catch less when the yellow fruit was on board. One more belief about bananas? That they'd bring along unwanted stowaways in the form of venomous spiders and snakes, which could potentially kill off a crew.

While not allowing women aboard ships is thankfully a thing of the past, the same can't be said for the beleaguered banana. Today, some sailors continue to leave bananas behind when they board a boat—even bypassing banana-scented sunscreen because of the superstition.

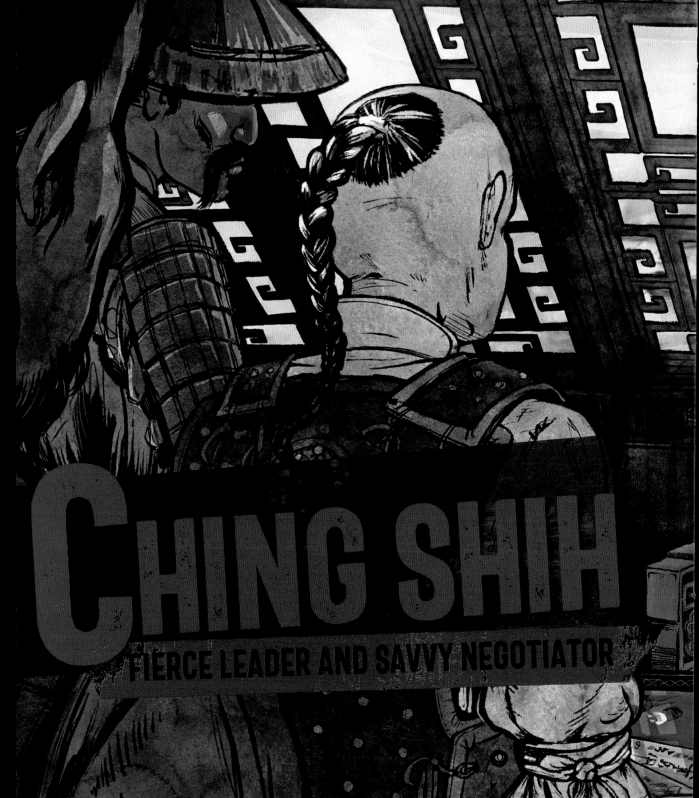

CHING SHIH

FIERCE LEADER AND SAVVY NEGOTIATOR

WHEN: ca A.D. 1775 to 1844 **WHERE:** South China Sea **WHO:** Ching Shih, whose masterful leadership made the massive Red Flag Fleet indomitable, commanded more ships and more pirates than any other pirate in history. **ALIAS:** Ching Shih aka Cheng I Sao aka Zheng Yi Sao aka Madame Ching. Traditional Chinese for "widow of Cheng": 鄭氏

THE PREEMINENT PIRATE

Ching Shih, the Pirate Queen,
was ruler of the seas.
She brought enemies, emperors,
and dynasties to their knees.

Not much is known about her youth.
Her birth name is a mystery.
The story of young Ching Shih's life?
Forever lost to history.

Legend says she toiled at sea
until one fateful day
a pirate captain fell in love
with Ching Shih's brilliant ways.

It's said that Cheng I hurriedly
asked Ching Shih for her hand.
I do, she said, as long as I am
equal in command.

They wed and shared their bounty.
They joined in love and war.
They terrorized the Chinese seas
as no one had before.

The King and Queen of bloodshed
ruled the Red Flag Fleet:
a ragtag band of pirates
impossible to beat.

When a tsunami slayed her husband,
Ching Shih's reign seemed done.
But she rose up to rule above
Cheng I's adopted son.

She wisely made Cheung Po Tsai
her trusty right-hand man.
He brutally ensured
the execution of her plans.

The Imperial Navy launched an attack,
sure of Ching Shih's demise.
She lured them in and took them out—
victory by surprise.

Raiding wealthy villages,
she demanded they pay dues,
and promised them protection
that no one dared refuse.

She put in place the strictest laws
that filled her crew with dread.
Disobey me? Off with your ears!
A second time? Your head!

Most female prisoners were set free.
No women were mistreated.
The men who disobeyed were killed—
mistakes were not repeated.

At Ching Shih's mighty peak,
she saw fame and fortune soar
to eighteen hundred ships—
more than any pirate had before.

From the narrow Strait of Malacca
to the sandy Yellow Sea,
she commandeered and conquered,
living in infamy.

Ching Shih, the Pirate Queen,
was ruler of the seas.
She brought enemies, emperors,
and dynasties to their knees.

COMMANDER IN CHIEF

SAILING THE **SOUTH CHINA SEA, CHING SHIH AND HER HUSBAND** SHARED COMMAND OF THE POWERFUL **RED FLAG FLEET.** AFTER HIS DEATH, CHING SHIH TOOK CHARGE OF THEIR FLEET, WHICH FLOURISHED INTO A POWERFUL PIRATING BUSINESS UNDER **HER RUTHLESS RULE.**

This historical painting shows what Canton, the region in China where Ching Shih lived and that she later raided as a pirate, looked like around 1800.

TAKING OVER

Ching Shih made history at the helm not with her birth name but with her husband's. They had been married for six years when he died suddenly. Ching Shih—or Cheng I Sao, as she was sometimes called, which means "wife of Cheng I"—commandeered their pirate business, supposedly telling her fleet, "We shall see how you prove yourselves under the hand of a woman."

DREAM TEAM

The convincing new commander persuaded rival pirates to work together under her leadership. As a result, she united an enormous squadron of an estimated 1,800 ships staffed with more than 80,000 pirates. She appointed her adopted son, Cheung Po Tsai, as captain of the fleet, freeing her to focus on business and military strategy. Before long, her pirates were not only pillaging and plundering at sea, but also expanding to schemes on land, such as extortion and blackmail. They also took over several coastal villages.

SHREWD MOVES

She's often called history's most successful pirate. So just how prosperous was Ching Shih? To put it in perspective, her fleet of 1,800 ships and 80,000 men was hundreds of times larger than other well-known raiders of the time, like Captain Blackbeard. Managing such a colossal fleet couldn't have been easy, and it's said that Ching Shih's business savvy, which she picked up before she married, helped her be a better boss. Aside from overseeing the day-to-day schedules of her own army of ruffians, she was able to devise military strategy, manage the financials of her fleet, and broker business deals. One of Ching Shih's most impressive alliances? Developing a partnership with local farmers, who agreed to supply her men with food. And with 80,000 mouths to feed, that deal was certainly no small potatoes.

As more money flowed in, Ching Shih set up a pirate's bank to ensure her crew had savings to support their families.

LAW AND ORDER

Ching Shih wrote a set of laws for her crew to follow, and those who broke them were severely punished. Anyone caught disobeying a superior's orders, for example, faced the threat of having their ears cut off—or worse, they'd be beheaded. Often, at sea, pirates would bring women aboard their ships as slaves. Ching Shih refused to allow this mistreatment. She mandated that male pirates could only bring their wives on board, and punished anyone who dared to mistreat them.

SOVEREIGN OF THE SEAS

By 1807, the Red Flag Fleet was more organized than the Chinese navy. Chinese officials tried to stop the fleet with the help of British and Portuguese warships, but the Red Flag Fleet defeated that armada. Outmaneuvered and outmanned at every turn, the Chinese government had no choice but to forgive Ching Shih's crimes. In exchange, they asked Ching Shih to stop pirating. She agreed, but on the condition that her entire crew be pardoned too.

She got what she wanted—along with a small fleet of ships for her husband to command, offers of military employment for her crew members, and money for their new life onshore. They also got to keep their loot.

A LEADER'S LEGACY

A life on land didn't mean laying low for Ching Shih. Instead, she used her fortune to start new business enterprises, which by all accounts were pretty successful. She died peacefully at the age of 69.

This shrewd commander from humble circumstances used her smarts and resourcefulness to create one of the most formidable pirate fleets the world has ever known.

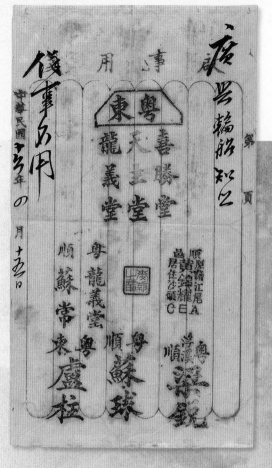

This painting on silk by an unknown artist shows what boats in the eastern seas around China looked like during Ching Shih's reign.

A FORCE TO BE RECKONED WITH

During the Qing dynasty, which lasted from 1644 to 1912, women were viewed as their husband's property. They were even born without a name of their own. Because women and men were not considered equals, women could not receive a proper education or own land. Instead, they were expected to fill the roles of wife and mother and to spend their days cooking and cleaning.

So how did Ching Shih become an exception to that rule? Marrying Cheng I, a famous captain from a long line of prosperous pirates, certainly helped. She took advantage of her proximity to power, supposedly demanding equal control of his pirate fleet as a condition of their marriage. When he died, she had to find a way to maintain her power, this time as sole leader.

She convinced Cheung Po Tsai (Cheng I's adopted son and the rightful heir to the throne) to marry her, and she gave him a job as the muscle of the ship. He did the dirty work while she remained head of operations, rising to a level of power never seen in a pirate before or since.

The story of each powerful pirate in this book has been written in verse, as a poem. You may be surprised to find out that there are countless different types of poetry, from sonnets (such as the ones Shakespeare wrote) to haiku, and many more, spanning languages and cultures. Some have strict rules that must be followed, such as the number of lines in the poem, rhyme patterns, or rhythm, while others have little to no limitations. But one thing all poems have in common is that they allow you to express your thoughts and feelings in wild, wonderful ways, and to write things that have never been written before. Check out the six verse forms that were used in this book—and take a stab at writing some poetry yourself!

"THE BATTLE OF SALAMIS": ARTEMISIA I OF CARIA

DOUBLE SONNET: A sonnet is a 14-line poem, usually written in lines of iambic pentameter (with a typical rhythm of "da-DUM, da-DUM, da-DUM, da-DUM, da-DUM), and following some specific rhyme pattern. "The Battle of Salamis" is a double sonnet, with two sets of 14 lines, following a nontraditional rhyme scheme of ABBACCDABBAEDE / FGGFHHIFGGFJIJ. Each letter represents the rhyme at the end of a line. All A's rhyme with other A's, all B's rhyme with other B's, and so on.

"I WILL BE QUEEN": SELA

DIALOGUE POEM: A dialogue poem often reflects a conversation between two people who represent opposing perspectives. When read aloud, it is intended to be voiced by different people, or read by the same person using different voices.

"KISMET": SAYYIDA AL HURRA

GHAZAL (pronounced "guzzle"): Originating from Arabic poetry, a ghazal is found in Middle Eastern and Indian literature and music. It is a lyric poem with a fixed number of verses and a repeated rhyme. Here are the rules of a ghazal:

a. 5 to 12 couplets, or *shers,* of equal metrical and/or syllabic length, though no meter is imposed.

b. No enjambments between the couplets. This means that each couplet must be complete, and not be continued onto the next line.

c. Each couplet should be able to stand as its own individual poem.

d. Both lines of the first couplet and the second line of each following couplet feature the same word or phrase at the end.

e. Both lines of the first couplet and the second line of each following couplet feature the same internal rhyme, located immediately before the repeated word or phrase.

f. The poet may choose to personalize the ghazal by quoting his or her name or nickname in the final couplet.

g. Traditionally, ghazals were only called "ghazal" and not given another title.

"PETITION TO QUEEN ELIZABETH I": GRACE O'MALLEY

EPISTOLARY POEM (also called a verse letter or letter poem): An epistolary poem is written in the form of a letter.

"THE ENDLESS FIGHT": ANNE BONNY

FREE VERSE: Free verse is an open form of poetry that does not follow any traditional rules such as consistent rhyme, meter, or stress patterns. However, poets may still use rhythm, rhyme, alliteration, and assonance to create powerful pieces.

"THE PREEMINENT PIRATE": CHING SHIH

BALLAD: A ballad tells a story using short stanzas, typically arranged in quatrains (sets of four lines) and using the ABAB or ABCB rhyme scheme. Ching Shih's poem follows the rhyme scheme of ABCB, then EFGF, and so on.

FOR ALL THE FEARLESS FEMALES WHO DESERVE TO HAVE THEIR STORIES TOLD,
NOT LEAST MY OWN CAPTIVATING CREW: SANAY, SELIS, AND TOLA —LL

Since 1888, the National Geographic Society has funded
more than 14,000 research, conservation, education,
and storytelling projects around the world. National
Geographic Partners distributes a portion of the funds
it receives from your purchase to National Geographic
Society to support programs including the conservation
of animals and their habitats. To learn more, visit
natgeo.com/info.

For more information, visit nationalgeographic.com,
call 1-877-873-6846, or write to the following address:

National Geographic Partners, LLC
1145 17th Street, N.W.
Washington, DC 20036-4688 U.S.A.

For librarians and teachers: nationalgeographic.com/
books/librarians-and-educators

More for kids from National Geographic: natgeokids.com

National Geographic Kids magazine inspires children
to explore their world with fun yet educational articles
on animals, science, nature, and more. Using fresh storytelling and amazing photography, *Nat Geo Kids* shows
kids ages 6 to 14 the fascinating truth about the world—
and why they should care. kids.nationalgeographic.com/
subscribe

For rights or permissions inquiries, please contact
National Geographic Books Subsidiary Rights:
bookrights@natgeo.com

Designed by Eva Absher-Schantz
Illustrations by Sara Gómez Woolley

Library of Congress Cataloging-in-Publication Data

Names: Lewis, Leigh, author.
Title: Pirate queens : dauntless women who dared to rule
    the high seas / Leigh Lewis.
Description: Washington, DC : National Geographic,
    [2022] | Audience: Ages 8-12 | Audience: Grades 4-6
Identifiers: LCCN 2021011540 | ISBN 9781426371950
    (hardcover) | ISBN 9781426371967 (library binding)
Subjects: LCSH: Women pirates--Biography--Juvenile
    literature. | Poetry--Juvenile literature. | Piracy--
    History--Juvenile literature.
Classification: LCC G535 .L495 2021 | DDC 910.4/5--dc23
LC record available at https://lccn.loc.gov/2021011540

The publisher acknowledges the team who made this
book possible: Paula Lee, Sarah Wassner Flynn, and
Rose Davidson, contributing writers and researchers;
Ariane Szu-Tu, editor; Lori Epstein, photo director;
Christina Ascani, photo editor; and Grace Hill Smith,
project manager. A special thanks to the panel of experts
and historians who vetted the book's content: David
Cordingly, Greg Fisher, Lin Foxhall, Vicki Szabo, Kathy
Fagan, the members of the SCBWI Ohio Central South
critique groups, the reference staff and librarians at
UAPL, and agent Elizabeth Harding. And lastly, to Daniel
A. Bean, who encouraged a young girl to love pirates.

Printed in China
21/RRDH/1